Poems Of Mirages And Miracles

Babar M. Saggu

For Bushra Owais

My wife, my dearest friend and in so many ways my mentor, critic and muse, most often at the same time, the courageous artist who stood by my work always and who has been a constant source of inspiration, to continue to explore my vision, art and creativity.

CONTENTS

Background

About a decade ago or more, Bushra and I tried to install or present these poems in various theater and performance art festivals in Lahore, in a conservative and conformist atmosphere of our native country Pakistan and failed.

I had strived to see these installation poems as I call them, put into action and installed as living and moving events of poetry and it is my hope that this pamphlet will serve as a template, for these and other such action poems and an invitation to other artists and poets who wish to use the format.

Some of my installation poems remained just notes, but it is important to us at this time to preserve some of my work.

You will notice a colored text, to facilitate distinct threads and pathways with suggestions or instructions where appropriate, the cardinal directions are not specified purposefully and instead the idea is to adapt to the space of performance or installation, with distinct pathways, distinct routes and turns, allowing the reader choices of which path one wishes to follow, or retrace and take another turn as in the first poem. Other installed poems are simpler although they also invite the reader to walk alongside a changing view of words.

It is my belief that we bring to art, to poetry and to our interactions with each other, that we bring to the world at large, the image, the speech or even our memory, our own experienced symbolic and interpretive, meaning making and individual color, we give it a new form just by looking or listening, even if it is infinitesimal a difference in comparison to the last time we looked at something or heard a narrative or shared time with another person. So as a poet, I have always seen my role to be a sieve, to allow for and build holes and spaces and lacunae of meaning , so that another may fill their own voice in, their thoughts, their colors, meanings and process.

To me poetry is alive and moving. The second part of this pamphlet includes my experimental work, which explores the boundaries of spoken word, performance and written poetry.

Installation Poems

The Poems Of Mirages And Miracles

<u>Preamble</u>

*To be arranged in labyrinths, spaces, patterns and lines
to be mounted or written on walls, to be spread, framed or nailed
into the ground, it's my vision visible to me in a reflective space, yes,
yes,
the poems change as you walk along them, lead to pictorial ends, or
emit sounds as you see and feel them, in the process of making my
vision, visible; I will
sculpt my eyes, and let you touch them,
or open my ears, so you can hear
the sounds of most simple meditations
that I have heard, I wish that you will freely explore,
that you will move in whichever direction, follow whichever phrase,
word, or sound and contemplate, that nothing is fixed in any
narrative, that we can re-tell, re-visit and renew our connections with
narrative and by extension our relational
and lived experiences.*

Poem # 1 - Help

To be printed on artist inkjet paper cut to 2"x 4" size strips (the text broken into panels as in these lines), glued in the center of cradled hardboard (Ampersand Hardbord) 6" x 6" x 3/4", to be mounted on walls, equidistant from each other, but at different heights as the lines dip up and down in this text, but this is not a rigid rule, rather we expect an aesthetic flow of waves of panels, as much the space allows for it. The panels initially move right or left, from the point of entrance. The left hand side (or depending on the space, right hand side) may then branch into further right and left (considered ahead and back), as the ahead/right space will lead to a wooded stool with a white-noise box placed on it, plugged in and running, while the back/left space will lead to an installation of 100 cradled hardboard panels and the printed text on it, all equidistant in a grid.
The next installed part can be continued from either the 100 panel installation or the white noise machine on a stool.

go right   and vanquish   the musings   the flowing moans   of your other self

slide as it comes   to you   bidding farewell
to moonlit   mother   hanging above your breast
hauling with it the   sand, the stars, the seven orbs of
wind

or go left

and be vanquished
by centuries
of doubt
and be, that which is
the question, unanswered

how do we form from
dust
and the cause
the cause   the cause
escapes us   again   go again   go   again

ahead right
and fall into your soul, sullied
belied
nailed to heavens
and hanging upside down
as the sign
you wore the day before your birth

(White noise machine on a wooden stool)

10

back left
through
your own projected divinity
heightened beyond your reach

and kneel before
the one hundred failed concepts

of your day

Installation of 100 panels – In random order – equidistant in a grid
Marx x 5 panels
Pleasure x 5 panels
Human x 5 panels
Love x 5 panels
Progress x 5 panels
Truth x 5 panels
Science x 5 panels
God x 5 panels
Equality x 5 panels
Migration x 5 panels
Empowerment x 5 panels
Capitalism x 5 panels
Idealism x 5 panels
Entertainment x 5 panels
Information x 5 panels
Democracy x 5 panels
Morality x 5 panels
Culture x 5 panels
Hospitality x 5 panels
Psychology x 5 panels

Extension: (either from the white noise machine or from the 100 panel installation)

afar from the shore   the traveler calls   back, ye
                                                                back
come back
I am left
back

and back

he goes to another slithering
life
on shore
as no one will have him
he will have no one
too

                              for
                               oh for
                                    oh forsaken my poor you
                                              come here
                                              and relive
                                                  be healed
                                                     shed your former
                                                         willing
                                                             diseased

shell and be

unwillingly subjugated

or become the cure

here
here
here
the cure
we have
the cure
gather here

for the very nature
                         of it
                            is surrounded by a found device
                                        of mass use.

A waist high pile of assorted newspaper with the word 'help' written on it with yellow
enamel paint, serves as the end point, preferably close to the exit from the installation.

Poem # 2 – The Visit

To be printed on artist inkjet paper cut to 2"x 4" size strips, glued on birch panels of progressively varying sizes, mounted on a wall, equidistant from each other and at the same (center) height from the floor.

slacken your tongue
hear no more
say no more
seal your eyes
seal your ears

I am here
here
here
here I am
I am here
here
here

(The panels get progressively smaller and then progressively get larger until they reach the same size as the initial panel)

here
here
I am here
here I am
here
here
I am here

I am

(A stone slate mounted on a wooden panel with a white circle drawn in centre with "I am" written in white enamel paint)

Poem # 3 – The Old Man Waiting

To be printed on paper, cut into 2"x 4" strips, to be glued on 6"x 6" birch panels, mounted on a wall in a square configuration, all panels equidistant from each other.

when
when
when will it
will it, when it won't
when will it
will it
it won't
or it will
and it won't
or it will and won't will it
when
when
will it, when it won't
when will it
will it, when it won't
when will it

Poem # 4 – Specters Of Marx

To be printed on paper, cut into 2"x 4" strips, to be glued on various sized birch panels, mounted on a wall, all panels equidistant from each other and at same height (center) from floor. From the first panel to the last the font of text as well as the size of birch panels will become progressively smaller.

as you read
your
shining eyes
gaze
into my
long gone out life

Experimental Work

Collage Poems/Cut-ups

These poems were composed by logrolling found words, the sources are trivial, an English newspaper published in Lahore, cut-up over three weeks at random and then rearranged, the subjects are feigned and the characters arbitrary, leaving behind free association and pure structure.

I
Seafarer

Forward, the commander would
once he turned
he would surf
fishtailing away
fatally destroying himself
on the ground crabbed
the pit crew shambles

I heard this big rumble
the tug tow gone and the starboards turns
fragments could so be dangerous
tough day tough day, he said
if the failing firm did damage the ship
losing a single man can do you in
awaiting a lift home aboard
loosen your fare

whether we will is impossible to know
a black hole
can sometimes grow too tired
to be brave

II

Asleep

Draw
breathe
drags
share the sweet
melancholic harsh salvation
as he tutors her
carelessly opening her thighs
covered in steam smelling tears
of confusion
the very definition of love and youth

crimes of quick witted
planning the name
you can see the forsaken look in his eyes
tracing her, by turns dervish and wanton
coming of age

III

Collogue

Dressed up
hair held high
blue beams of
formed and marketed
would be, could now be
dirty old men
trickling down their blouses
honest about ourselves
and the actual sex
cycling or two inside our first
domesticated vanquisher
made to shock their pandering brass bones out
of their popping eyes

a caress is worth three
a kiss just free and if you won't have it
our way of sticking it out
let's part, part now and be
nice song, right, right song
as the rebellious
positions empty and the chair moves on
we will at once discard this outrage
your vote for our love
our love for you and yours

IV

Conflict

He would
down on
unless down
and it would take
we_are_waiting
to see hope
to see we are waiting

V

Lullaby

For the loved companion on a sleepless night

Such a world in such a word is wasted
Such a word in such a world is wasted

Poetry as Pointillism

Playing hand for hand

Studies in impressionism, breaking methods, truncating scenes and characters and resounding moments in which pure ideas sound vibrantly, for all else is silence and that which is contained is contained herein, nothing thereafter, for I am varied, and my glance seals my sordid bitter memory in varying shades to project a film through my translucent eyes, upon my eyes.

One

on top-
black cat-for it is a black and white-
like the sheen of sweat on her shoulders
as he stares-between the threads-like the
and below-
dancing with the newborn held high
in arms-
far below-
tin caps scrapping off the stairway
hell cuts open-

curtains draw and a great squeal of joy
pierces every head-
they run up-they
run down
they- make up
slash-triadhighmakc-mc jump
pet you-pet them-drunk-them drunk-them
dunces
sweet ye sew ye sew on sew on-yea
dunk you hey-you dunk them slunk slip them
slippers
kiss ye kiss um make em new babes tonight
we might

now ladies idle along-idle along the dial
for in a moment or two
it strikes half past moon red
and it is time for bed

now a storey higher nigh a storey less
day past's fretters press

for another day in mansions of joy may
mention
another toy for your sublime life about-rising
and falling-
black and white

Two

sail mother sail
victors
to their perch and veil
the dying more
the horizon behind your pinned up hair
flaming- torches- corpses
oh-die
you forgot-
my little son forget forget my son
mother forget my little son-who
in set eyes and raw flesh-lay wise
wise-suffocating-wise as he silences your ego
into blameless forgetfulness

Three

two gleaming buttons
identical
wait for a single loop to pass over their necks
and strangulate them

Four

tantalum chained to timber veins
bulging across his temples
this primitive man gropes his way
leading million year ordeals of vouchsafed
brevity
through slave-man-of-man-of-slave-of-
laughter-of-civilization-of-truth

Five

redo
row and row again through
disillusionments
fighting all harm
and will-be done
for

Six

it strikes nine
and the chaperon in the painting in the
mirror
yawns as girls behind
indifferent, radiant and smiling
wash their legs and walk away to caresses
one after the other
what if one was allowed to turn ones neck
only still

Seven

this is seven, and so to be, as numbers
and storm and that to be the storm play
with the blue winged angel

a slight disease overtakes him
and he
passes out

now come to
worshipful white loincloth

and live or die

carcass run among the branching
and you stare
your hair mangled
so close to my worldly eye that
I cannot see you

and my eye in its grasp
I gaze
the future marching by me
feather and paws

blood and spit
rusting
hoe and sickle

Eight

but
her mother covets
plastic flowers more
than those in
the garden

Nine

where she bows and her
head
light struck
strikes the ground
where two rivers split
man and woman
torrent and ripple
where two rivers join
moon with its light and earth in its shade
where two gleaming glances sideways cross
grass in its whispers and wind in its touch
where two petting hands in their motions
greed
life in its thaw and death in its life
your forms begin and end with a single red
colored reed
pendulous against your breasts
resting on your thighs

bent in wise thoughtfulness
and a prayer

Ten

her face
a
clock
set
in
timely jewels
her eyes
orbs
of unforgiving
rays of felicity
her two mirthful sprites
mingle
within a singular gaze
full of stars
burst into song

the song ___

for a stoop went the filthy rich of heart and poor of soul a blaming the monstrous visage in his head while on the same idylls he had suckled and on the same life he had wasted himself and on the same note of propriety had he exerted all his righteousness and piety and in most pitiful way had he fallen a short of the leaf as it filled its gullet with a poisonous spray, on and this Dionysian day as Apollo slept in his armory and sprayed it on its sly prey, the monstrous images stooped again and once for the twinkle of a second the brimming seemed to be a brim, but will it be that its be done and it be as it is to be, will you my love, be so unforgiving, as it is, that you will not overlook, that I sought no solace for you, yet I am pleased to be it for you, but as it is, I am a part of that which is larger than I am, and it seeks all it seeks for you, before that whole of which I am a part, you stand blameless, for it will rather have the blame than have you blame yourself, but I am as it is, a servile villainous man, a cotton bale that has been compressed all it can for

want of more by its own selfishness, but I recognize, I could have made it, by saying, I am responsible, and that I be forgiven, but I did not, and now, it is not I, it's the greater, the larger of which I am a part, it is the whole world and its word, songbirds and flowers and haystacks, that wishes to be forgiven in my place, it is the sticks and the grass, the ants and the willow, the leopards and the salmon, the tortoise and the thorn bush, the maddened crew and the sail and the mast, the morning as it breaks when love dawns and the night that falls when flesh which made love possible dies away, withers and falls out of existence and truth that it was beholden to in its day, the plough and the creepers that dread its claw, the ash and the dust, all these, of which I am made, ask forgiveness in my place.

Eleven

a lute
four boots
underclothes
a pair of socks
a man and a woman
and thirty bullet shells within the ditch
flowing
red
red
red

brittle
beetles
scattered on the floor

two hundred
I count
two hundred

brittle beetles
and a fragile woman
some pieces of glass

Twelve

'he has locked himself in'

take a chalk
draw a circle
move around it
but not inside

'two pantomimes'

stay stray
bad mad

'will you come out now'

no
now
no

'she is gone'

counting her steps
seventy one, two, three
far away, far
far away

Poetry As Performance

Introduction:

A simple deviation of sense is pine wood and winter while the crudity of knowledge that I possess is overwhelming.
I have a free standing notion of my reality even if there are illusions.
Some might dream while there is no need to say it, there really is no need to stand about and listen, coming and passing through, returning and gazing, we all move on.
One morning he said while we were driving, "how far will we", and then broke off, substantial proof of everything if you ask me, "how far will we".
Someone might have breathed soothing words into his cut ear.

Invisibility:

Do you see me?
No you don't
I see you cannot see me

The names of things:

Flourishing
Human
Life like light
Death

Visible vision:

This is an image.
That is a mirror reflecting it.
Now we will enter a dark fantasy.
Will you close your eyes?
There is no one else.

Her double:

The screen shows the performer's face, with a white bandage wrapped around her lower face, facing a mirror. Teeth and exposed gums have been painted on this demi-mask on the right hand side.

She has some red fluid pouring down her face and neck. She will face her own image in a mirror and she will whisper in a dialogue, silent, but forced with gestures of the upper face and with slow corporeal juxtapositions of limbs and neck, such that every movement corresponds to the length of the spoken word dialogue.

Dialogue for male & female voices:

Did he?

        Such as this is possible, without a cause for cause

He will

        Closed behind the curtains a fall

Look closer

        He is a bastard and his…

Come here at once

        You are dangerous to yourself, which is most dangerous

I am surreptitious

        You swine, look somewhere else

Dialogue for female voice only:

Time

    Death

Urge

    Sex

Bliss

    Death

Sex

    Mother

Fraud

    Shit

Freud

    Father

Future

    Death

Wish

Wish?….. (Questioningly)
Wish? ….. (Wistfully)
Wish?….. (Annoyed)

An emotion every ten steps:

The male and female actor take ten steps, each one of them with their right hand before their face, every tenth step an emotion is displayed just by facial expression as the actor removes their hand from before their face.

Lights Out:

If you are finished here, you may leave.
Or we can all listen to whatever someone has to say.
It is an indeterminate experience.
Please sit down, wherever you are now.
Don't fear whoever is around you.
We are all strangers and we might believe in different things but we are incapable of anything inhuman.
An accident may occur, someone may cast us out.
We will still remain human and our cruelty to each other is no more than our silence. Now, who was John Cage, for I doubt we know him any more than we know about music.
Silence
Please speak, or feel free to leave.
Silence, while one or more people speak.
Silence until the audience leaves.

Poetry as Text

A singular projection

0-1-2

These pages are intended to be an extension of my present self and its beliefs, their implications and limitations, the formal legacy of which I have received from reading of history itself, or from the phrase, the phrase itself meaning in its defining form to be a divination handed down by an obscure number of characters, or in its subtlety to be the product of additions and subtractions by any number of characters in time before me, that being the only thing known to me by reflection and the activity itself a part of many reflective associations learned over time **0**, *all the while knowing and fearing that it is not the act of writing but a grappling with the act of intending to write and instead grappling with the act of grappling with the intending.* **1**

It is constructed in an unusual way, the sentence, but that is the best I can think of, and that on many tries **2**. As it happens that the preceding sentence about the sentence preceding that sentence is constructed, I write it down, thinking all the time about the next sentence to be constructed, and this happens that the next sentence again is about the preceding sentence, and also the one preceding that. I think, I have a deliberation to make, here at this point, while I am grappling with the beginnings of an idea and writing it, that being, the making of the sentences, how are these sentences made, but even before that I will make another digression, that being, how are they linked, and answering this, I will return to the construction of sentence 1, which itself is the reason why sentence **2** was constructed, and then the sentence **2** was reflective, and as I continued this reflection this led to sentence number **3** and so forth.

This gives us answer to a question that has not been asked as yet, the subject of the sentences, the subject of a sentence under construction, thus cannot be too far removed from the *Proximity* of a sentence already formed in our mind. Similarly all subjects of thought that follow one another and can be called as thinking itself are contained within a *Closure* that being in close proximity to each other.

These pages are intended to be an extension of my present self that is bound by closure, and this closure, leads to a streamlined choice of words, far removed from their context, and not integrated by a sense of oncoming, this oncoming being the struggle to relate to the next sentence. This must explain, the solitary choice of words, itself a product of struggle to escape the closure and the reflexive nature of this process.

3-
I have intended this sentence to be different.

4-5
The intention itself is contingent upon preceding matters, as for this sentence it is closed up by 3 and putting together two ideas gives it a continuity, the "and" being the conjoining word, thus intention unfolds before us as a consequence too not a cause alone.

6
At all times, the word and its implied meanings have not been constant, this much can be used to illustrate, as a beginning of wayward exponential theorizing, *imagism*, the art and motives as related to their motifs, while not as the driving need behind their work or the pioneering urge to free verse from bondage at that time visible and perceived, are by and large related to a use of exacting language by the various members of this movement, not the almost near or nearly exact and decorative use but the exact one and such a form of poetry, while we will at length describe our heartfelt and otherwise about poetry, we will tend to stay closer to the scope of imagist ideal by starting with an effort to use the best words.

First to use the word exactly one must know the right word and this may lead to another trial that of finding the word. Why a trial for it stands as a synonym tested and examined and also as an ordeal of language. To find the word one tries it against what one feels is true and befitting to the circumstance one is in, and subjectivity, that too enclosed, can in this instance be called ability. This ideal is further limited by the variable presence of words in closure and in a larger picture the knowledge of the one intending to find the word or on the ability of recalling itself.

This trial that one faces renders one susceptible to self appraisal and judgment that may range from finding oneself innocent to the extent of incapacitation. I shall now illustrate two instances of the same. One from colloquial usage of naiveté and another from an artistic juxtaposition of inability

I have no words, can be posited as an expression of innocence leading to wonderment, while this lack of words, severely positions one's catastrophic knowledge of lack of knowledge close to unyielding dismay.

Now the word if used to illustrate words is categorical and in turn essential, for the knowledge of it is a common occurrence and can be relied upon as a tool to successfully render one's meaning, while usage defines what will appear to be novel to have the word coupled with another, that of rare usage or popularity will generate a wide array of expressions communicable. This word if unheard, the word unheard will have to it only one quality, music and this shall be taken as *opine* for in practice, many generate volitions that were not apparent before we exerted ourselves to find the exact word, in this case, at least non-imagist but closer to the ideal of it, for every word found is a found word and a source of wonderment and joy for the poet.

Apart from the express happiness of expression, to imagism there are values of freedom of subject, although to my taste this has ripened into a freedom from subject. The subject, apparent only in retrospect or on trial and inspection is the subject itself. The subject being its own subject is another replication of the found beat, that of reflection and concurrence. Whence we enter the explanation of subjects, from a particularly imagist point of view this becomes a point, where the poet may flourish his own hand and put the words, he so longingly strived to achieve, to the service of his present condition, that of poetry itself. In freely choosing the subject, he strives to render the closed words, ordinary in their own right, but contextually stirring and beautiful, into felt emotions such that a new air is born out of a new tune and not its opposite, but this seeming mirroring of ideals is unachievable, even when one cuts off from tradition completely.

This has resolved itself again in inability, but then one has another tool at hand, descriptive nature of truth, presentation of an image, such that no detail is redundant and none is false or used decoratively to masquerade the severity of its nature, the ugliness ugly and the beauty beautiful. This property of imagism can be called indiscriminate if the poet's own nerve does not imply the good or evil hence manifest in the word, but if one accepts the given-ness of it. Image as a word strives to reach the visibility of an image while its affliction arises from the difference in perceptive perspectives. Other than achieving specificity one can much less attain the quality of illustration but as a principle generalities are avoided using the imagist ideal of detail. A final element of economy of language then falls in discord with the formal preponderance of imagism and can only be achieved by cutting short some of the particulars, most of all, the ones commonly known or attributed to a subject, for such is a property of poetry that it goes only to the length of specificity that is novel in character which at most times is decorative, without its being an express cosmic value of usage but a solitary pondering of one linear imagination.

Then just as no birth occurs from the word birth itself and every and each is a recurrence of each and every occurrence past we will surmise by saying that the word unheard is the word worthy of its record, for within one and outside, there is forgetting and all art at the expense of being recursive exerts itself against this forgetting, such that some things may find their way into the future and in doing so the poet shuffles every thing's perspectives such that they do not loose their fondness of being found again and again, the ideals of imagism are imagined and here manifest themselves in critique while they may otherwise become a poem.

7

Criticism, as a literary tool is an effort to arrive at the same ends as may be achieved by the subject of critique and not the trial of the subject under study or an effort to achieve the implied or inherent meanings of a text under criticism. A movement towards replication of the ideal is not my purpose nor is making the study or the studied text transparent but I shall try to find what can be found within this discourse and outside, the relevance of which changes from time to time, thus this text structurally varies between discursive theorizing and critical analyses, both of its own structure and literary issues, on the whole issuing no single end in mind, thus exploring only exploration. In this land, as of all other literature one of the many tools language applies to its prime users, the poets is a sense of newness, in attempting to find newer expressions they tend to formulate combinations of words not combinations of realities, this fantastic approach arises from the feeling of inadequacy in both colloquial and poetic usage and repetitions interspersed with perspective. By perspective here we mean a transition of language and of course of expression, if spoken, of perception if heard or read from everyday saying to saying the formed word and thus raising it to a formality, a *saying* nonetheless. This appreciable gloss is a feeling often thought of as a visitation, reverie, caprice or poesy in any way, when one finds oneself capable of a *saying* and not just saying something. The poet now in turn, of having found in himself an impulse falls short of the structural elements of language, for language now after having led him this far no longer can serve his intention or intensity of emotion. This is when we encounter the established rules of the game and traditions, *Inversion* being one of them. A simple rearrangement of syntax for many a time seems enough, until one is able to see through it. One of the virtues of imagists was their understanding of the afforded ease of language at hands of a will to express and its smallish effects. The inversions then over took the purpose of the subject and provided momentary satisfaction but not without the fleeting stability of newness, but they themselves traded it for vividness of imagination or of observation. Now that the sated poet speaks, he says nothing, for all language is spent and only new way of creating is by destroying the older one, this at a structure-less present will do, but for the future one will need to find reflection super reflection and thence a resolve into simplicity, the implied beginning from where it all started and copied itself onwards and on.

This seems to be a grim end for textual practices, but our meager means do not allow us to dwell furthermore in this place and we shall move onwards towards other subjects, while we lasted and spent some mention of this particular form of poetry here only to begin with, but not to conclude, as for subjects there will be many interspersed with other issuing relevancies and irrelevancies, but on the whole, this shall explore my many intentions to explore language for the least and for the most expression itself and language.

By slightly touching the matter of inversion, I meant to illustrate that I have inklings of the way this text is being structured, not for good or for bad but for the matter that I do not have any easier means of elaboration right at hand and that I have just in the same way a poet does, invert and resolve, cut and prime his text, learned to express myself, most freely in this manner and I do not consider it an end but just a beginning towards my most vexed urge of creating a self examining textual practice and eventually an expansive self examining text or at least self aware of its implications and manifesting some choice as a means to freedom from closure and casual causality.

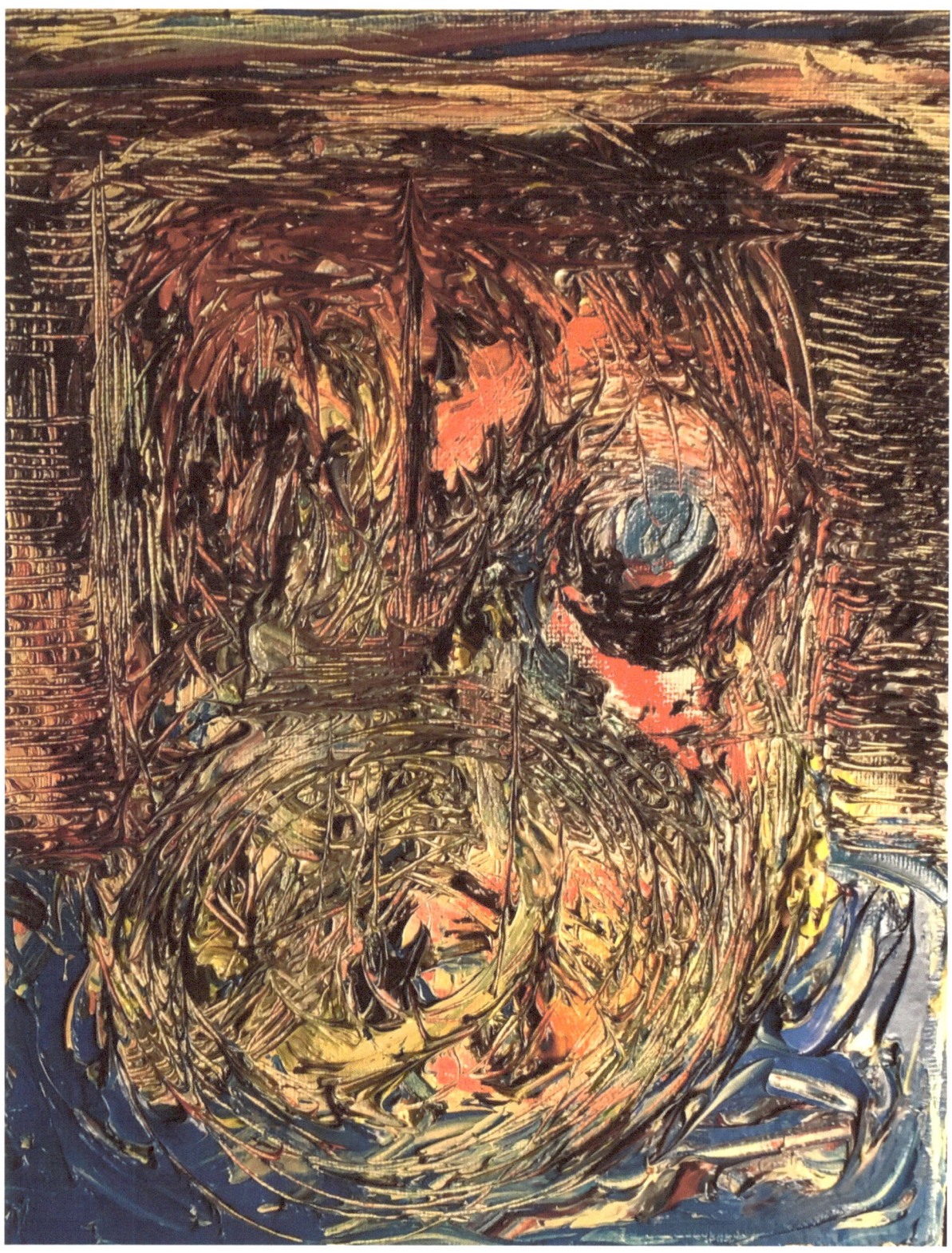

Cover image: Fire at the river crossing. Oil on canvas by the author

ABOUT THE AUTHOR

Babar M. Saggu, MD is a student of neuroscience and clinical research, working as a psychiatrist & psychodynamic psychotherapist, serving adults, children and adolescents, in New York, where he lives with his wife and a cat.

These editions of books, represent an effort to preserve Babar's work, by his friends and family in a time of turmoil, illness and adversity. He has written prolifically and the last fifteen or more years of his work span a range of experimental fictions, prose poems, poetry and plays.

He writes in three languages, Urdu, Seraiki and English, always looking to push the boundaries of expression, but he has kept his work to himself and a small circle of friends, with the understanding that although it does illuminate some things for himself, the narratives he has written may not represent more than the use of a free flowing, reflective space, of stream of conscious writing useful for self discovery and in turn relatedness with his loved ones.

www.ingramcontent.com/pod-product-compliance
Lightning Source LLC
Chambersburg PA
CBHW041318180526
45172CB00004B/1151

ISBN 9781544922287

90000 >

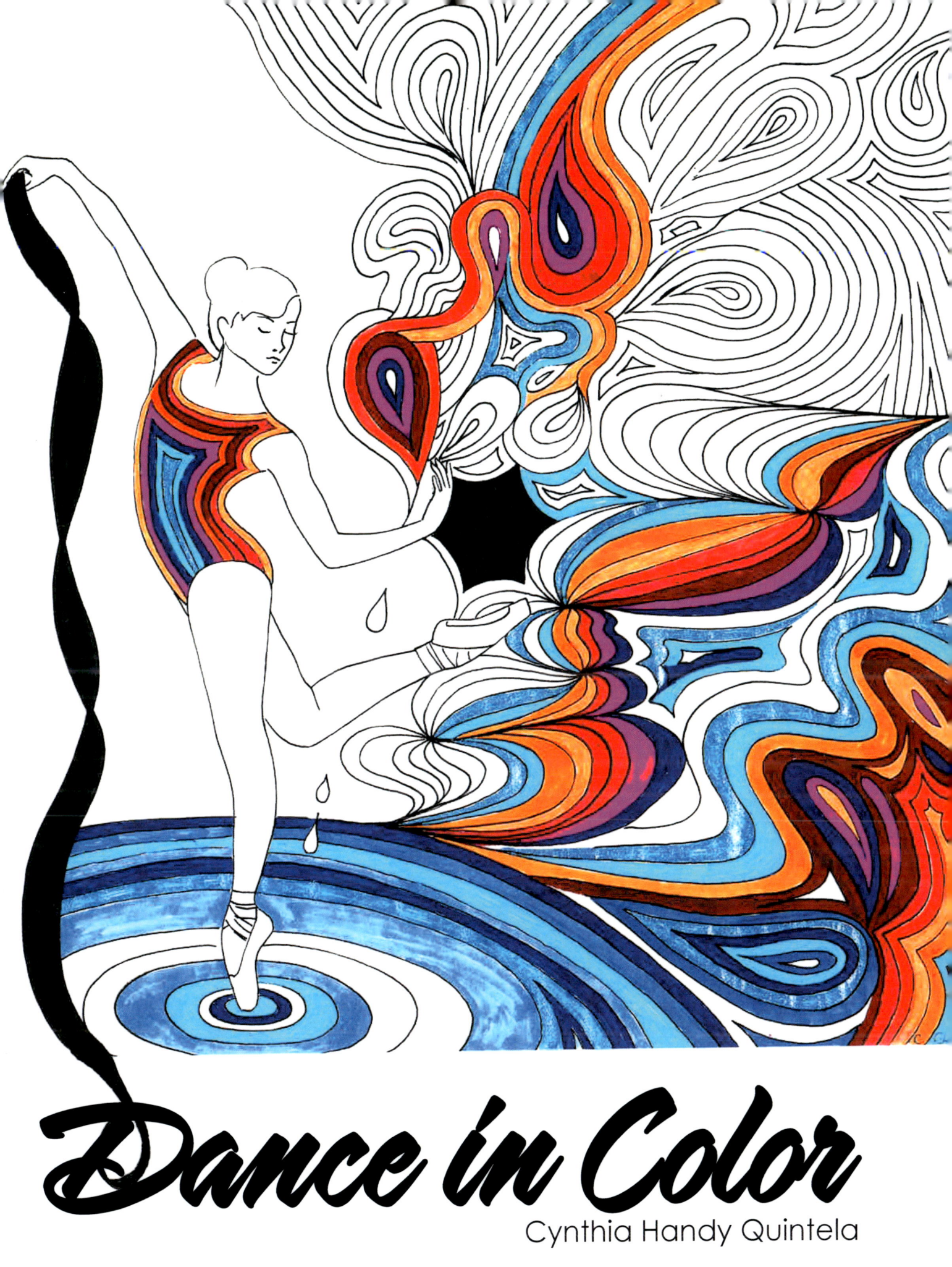

Dance in Color

Cynthia Handy Quintela